Osprey Modelling • 44

# Displaying your model

Richard Windrow

*Consultant editor* Robert Oehler

First published in Great Britain in 2009 by Osprey Publishing
Midland House, West Way, Botley, Oxford OX2 0PH, UK
443 Park Avenue South, New York, NY 10016, USA
E-mail: info@ospreypublishing.com

A CIP catalogue record for this book is available from the British Library.

ISBN: 978 1 84603 416 9
E-book ISBN: 978 1 84908 127 6

Editorial by Ilios Publishing Ltd, Oxford, UK (www.iliospublishing.com)
Design by Servis Filmsetting Ltd, Manchester, UK
Typeset in GillSans and 1Stone Serif
Index by Michael Forder
Originated by PPS Grasmere Ltd Leeds, UK
Printed in China through Bookbuilders

09 10 11 12 13 10 9 8 7 6 5 4 3 2 1

FOR A CATALOGUE OF ALL BOOKS PUBLISHED BY OSPREY MILITARY
AND AVIATION PLEASE CONTACT:

NORTH AMERICA
Osprey Direct, c/o Random House Distribution Center, 400 Hahn Road,
Westminster,MD21157
E-mail: uscustomerservice@ospreypublishing.com

ALL OTHER REGIONS
Osprey Direct, The Book Service Ltd, Distribution Centre, Colchester Road,
Frating Green, Colchester, Essex CO7 7DW
E-mail: customerservice@ospreypublishing.com

www.ospreypublishing.com

## Dedication

This book is dedicated to those stalwart members of the
'Saturday Morning Breakfast Club', Charles, David and Ramon,
without whose help I'm sure it would have been finished in half
the time.

## Photo credits

Except where credited otherwise, all photographs are
the author's

## Acknowledgements

During the preparation of this book a large number of people
have been most generous with their skills, allowing me to make
use of many of their photographs and, in some cases, putting up
with my disrupting their daily lives by letting me come into their
homes to take some of the pictures myself. I would like to record
my sincere thanks to them all here: (in alphabetical order) Haris
Ali, John Burnham, Charles Davis, Michael Fichtenmayer, Johan
Fohlin, Chris Grove, Rob Hendon, Mrs Roy Hunt, Geoffrey Illsley,
David Irving-James, Ken Jones of *Military Modelling*, Bryan Krueger,
Dave Maddox, Ernie Mirfin, 'Spud' Murphy of *Model Military
International*, Marcus Nicholls of *Tamiya Model Magazine
International*, Jaume Ortiz, Sheperd Paine, Spencer Pollard of
*Military in Scale*, Mike Rinaldi of *ModelX*, Mike Taylor, Antonio
Martin Tello, and last but by no means least Steve Zaloga. Many
thanks also to Marcus and Nikolai at Ilios Publishing for patiently
answering my technical queries. I also want to offer my sincere
thanks to my editor, Martin Windrow, for once again making my
work fit to appear before a discerning audience!

# Contents

# Approaches and choices

I think I should start by saying that in this book I'm setting out to achieve the rather difficult task of creating a work that will be of help, or at least of interest, to a wide readership ranging from the beginner to the more experienced modeller. Many of us build models just for the fun of it, and then put them on a shelf and derive pleasure from simply looking at them, but now and then we get the urge to enter one in a competition and have our work judged by our peers. Whether this is a local club event, a large national show or even an international such as EuroMilitaire, that is the moment when we want our model – figure, vignette or diorama – to be presented in the best way.

The choices we make about how the model is to be 'displayed' obviously cannot be a separate afterthought, and should usually be integral to the planning of the piece from the early stages. They can add to the appeal even of a single figure or vehicle, and become more important the larger the vignette or diorama is to be. An added dimension over recent years is the question of model photography, which is itself a type of 'display'. Nowadays quite sophisticated digital photographic effects are increasingly available and affordable, and while I have not gone into technicalities in this book the presentation of some of the photos provided for it by fellow modellers makes this relevant.

Naturally, the expert show-modellers amongst you don't need to be told how to get the best results; but this leaves a fairly large group of people, including myself, who are quite often looking for a new slant on how to finish and present a miniaturized piece of the real world. It never ceases to amaze me, when visiting shows such EuroMilitaire, to see how many variations on the basic theme modellers come up with – after all, there are only so many ways of doing this, between the extremes of a single figure on a simple plinth base and an ambitious diorama. The trick is to marry a particular model subject or treatment with a sympathetic method for displaying your work. There are always exceptions, but the mark of success is usually that your choice should not draw too much attention to itself (and it will, if you get it spectacularly wrong). Showing is a lot easier than describing, so I have included a gallery of pieces by both well-known and not-so-well-known modellers which might inspire some ideas for your next project. Not all of the illustrated examples are 'military', but the same principles obviously apply to all types of subject. The secondary purpose is to try to steer some of you to helpful suppliers, websites and products; many of the recommendations are based upon my own or fellow-modellers' experience and in most cases they have been used by modellers of all levels of expertise.

## General thoughts: dioramas

When talking about dioramas I'm assuming, for the purposes of this book, that the model subject itself has been finished and is now being set up for display. In most cases, of course, a diorama is not just a base on which to display a model (though naturally there is no reason why diorama techniques cannot be used simply for this primary purpose). But dioramas, perhaps more than any other type of modelling display, represent a frozen moment in time that enables the modeller to tell a story visually – to set a small piece of the real world in miniature. This can be fascinating for viewers of all ages, and even if the particular subject matter may not be of great interest to them they will still pore over the detail and admire the skill of the modeller. A few of the pictures I have included in this book are from dioramas, cutaway models and boxed scenes that

I have built for my friend Gerry Embleton, of Time Machine AG in Switzerland, to accompany the full-sized historical figures that he creates for museums in Europe and beyond. Gerry has always maintained that models complement larger exhibits, particularly for the children who may have rather less interest in those exhibits that appeal to their parents. A model of a Bronze Age woodcutter at work is going to be much more interesting for them than simply seeing his axehead in a glass case.

Among the most basic considerations is the angle from which your diorama is to be viewed. If it is to be seen only from the front (rather like a 3D photograph) then obviously any buildings or scenery need only be detailed from that viewpoint; but if the viewer can see either side of, say, part of a house, then the detailing must continue around the sides. This may seem too obvious to be worth stating, but I have seen dioramas that, although meant to be viewed from more than one angle, have all the detail confined to the front view and leave the sides or ends finished with distractingly less care. The diorama that I built of the Afrika Korps figures in some remote part of the North African desert ('Ozymandias', pages 9–15) was intended to be viewed from the front, with the giant face of the statue pulling the viewer's eye straight to the main point of the scene. So the model has just a sheet of wood at the back to cover the polystyrene blocks that form the basis of the piece, and a simple 'rock' finish around both sides, and the whole thing was then set in a horizontal 'picture frame' of polished wood.

This is the simplest style of display; some dioramas that I've seen have much more imaginative finishes. For instance, I remember one displayed at EuroMilitaire whose 'frame' was a large cutaway model of a bomb, enclosing a model B-17 Flying Fortress; and I have included one example (on page 70), set in an 'open book' effect, that is highly original. The only real limitations are your imagination and skill; however, I would suggest that you don't get so carried away with elaborating the method of display that the 'frame' overpowers the 'picture' – after all, the viewer is supposed to be admiring your modelling skills, not your carpentry.

One piece of advice on dioramas that you often hear is never to place the model on the groundwork dead centre and parallel to the front edge. In nearly every case this is correct; just as a photo or painting is best composed or cropped asymmetrically, so setting a modelled scene at an angle – with, say, an obliquely positioned track or hedgeline – is both more welcoming to the eye and can help draw the viewer's attention to that part of the model that is most important to you. However, no rules are cast in stone; particularly in cases where you wish to control a single viewpoint, the effect you want may best be achieved by a straightforward 'proscenium arch' presentation with the model sitting centrally.

Whether the diorama is composed to be seen head-on or obliquely, the cut-off or natural 'backstop' for the viewer's eye also needs to be considered; in other words, you want to control not only the angle at which the viewer sees your work, but also the 'focal depth'. It's a good idea, wherever possible, to have something at the back of a scene to act as such a visual backstop, be it a pile of rocks, a band of trees or a building. My 'Ozymandias' diorama was meant to be viewed from the front only, so the ruined wall along the top of the rockface makes a good visual cut-off and concentrates the viewer's attention on the action in the foreground.

## Boxed dioramas

When you build a boxed diorama the first steps taken are the same as for any other diorama: planning the positions of buildings, vehicles and figures, and either making a sketch plan to use as your guide or marking the positions on the baseboard/groundwork before you start. It can also be helpful to mock up buildings and vehicles with cardboard to ensure that your spacing is correct and that it will all fit when assembled.

Probably the greatest advantage of the boxed diorama is that you can control the lighting – the lighting in your room, or in the competition room at a show, may well not illuminate your model to its best advantage (for instance, if you wanted to recreate a night scene), but if the model is boxed then you can portray day, night, or anything in between. If the scene is an interior – of a room, an aircraft fuselage, or any other enclosed space – then you can just build your model and set it in the display box. The view of a room interior can be made to look more interesting if you angle the scene slightly within the outer box (see 'Light Boxes', page 31).

However, if the scene is set in the open air the question of perspective is more complex. The book on my shelf which has been of the greatest help to me when planning such work is *The Art of the Diorama* by Ray Anderson; this was published by Kalmbach Publishing in the USA in the 1980s, but if you are thinking of tackling this type of display for the first time it will certainly be worth your while to hunt down a second-hand copy.

If the back edge of the model is supposed to be at some distance from the viewer then you can use a painted backdrop with the model set in front, but with two particular provisos: firstly, the model must block off any view of a joint between the 'floor' and the 'back wall'; and secondly, any lighting you install needs to erase any shadow of the model on the back wall, otherwise your illusion of distance is destroyed. If the distance from viewer to 'horizon' is supposed to be considerable, then you can best achieve this effect by making the groundwork drop away in steps from front to back, so that it appears as though there is 'dead ground' between each step. You can also use vehicles or figures that gradually diminish in scale to give a greater illusion of distance (see 'False perspective', page 42). Assuming that the back wall will be mostly 'sky', paint this onto a curved length of card or thin sandwich board, and bring it round at each end to meet the inside face of the front of your box so that no corners show at the back. This may sound a bit complicated but once you try it you'll find it's not so bad, and of course it gives you the added advantage of obliging the viewer to look at the scene from your chosen viewpoint.

## Vignettes

A diorama allows for as much detail and action as you want, but a striking and sympathetic display for a model does not have to be huge. If, like me, you live in a flat, shelf space is probably at a premium, and your display options could be fairly limited; but this still allows for single figures, vignettes and small dioramas (either with or without domes and display cases, depending on whether or not it is you who is going to be doing the dusting). Display cases can even be bought with mirrored backs and bases so that a complete all-round view – including even the underside, suspension, etc. of the model truck or F1 racing car – can be appreciated.

If a substantial diorama is out of the question, a surprising amount of detail and intensity of action can be shown in a vignette; just a couple of figures or one vehicle and some detailed groundwork can still tell a story. When it comes to figures I'm at a disadvantage, since I'm not a figure painter and can only stand in awe of those of you who are. So many of the figures that I've seen at EuroMilitaire and in private collections leave me wondering if I'm in the right hobby; however, speaking as a viewer rather than a modeller, I have always found even single figures more striking if set in a small portion of scenery, whether groundwork or part of an interior. Once again, you get the impression of a tiny piece of the real world. (For an example of this, see the late Roy Hunt's striking piece 'God's Children' on page 50 – a world of fear, pain and tragedy all contained in a few square inches.)

*Basic materials and tools*
Note that information on how to contact companies supplying bases and display cases, a wide range of tools, materials, accessories and reference books can be

Tamiya has brought out a number of beginners' kits for those just starting out on modelling military vignettes; these 'before and after' photos are self-explanatory. (Photos and model by Robert Doepp, courtesy *Tamiya Magazine*)

found in the Appendix at the end of this book. I have also listed a number of websites – both of shops and companies that sell modelling equipment, and of useful modelling forums on which you can research your particular interest.

The baseboard for your diorama can be wood, marine plywood or Plexiglas or polystyrene blocks. The latter tends to be my preference these days, but if you choose wood or plywood then I would suggest that you paint both surfaces – in the past, when I have forgotten to do this, the board has subsequently warped when I've added a layer of plaster or Claycrete for my groundwork (see Steve Zaloga's model jeep on page 61). For my groundwork I prefer to use Claycrete (also called 'Celluclay'), which is a type of instant papier mâché to which you simply need to add water (with the groundwork colour already mixed in). Some modellers don't like this material as they have found that it sometimes cracks when completely dry; adding some PVA white glue to the mix will avoid this problem, although it does extend the drying time a bit. An added advantage with this material is that any 'leftovers' can be kept in a covered container and will remain usable for at least a week. Another reason I prefer Claycrete is that it dries with a texture to it, giving the impression of naturally rough ground, which is preferable to the smooth finish you get with plaster or modelling clay.

Once the basic groundwork is dry you then have a virtually unlimited range of products to choose from for the foliage, trees, water, rocks, stones, and myriad other items that can be used to create your miniature world. There are far too many to list, but I hope the Appendix is wide-ranging enough to enable you to find what you need.

For adhesives I mostly use exterior PVA white glue, which can be watered down if required, but on occasion I will use superglue. For spraying adhesive over a large area I use Woodland Scenics' scenic cement. Paints must be a matter of personal choice; I normally use Vallejo Acrylic Model Color but also, for certain detailing, oil paints and drawing inks.

The basic tools needed for building a diorama are as follows: a good quality scalpel or modelling knife, say Swan Morton or X-Acto, which can accept a number of different-sized blades; a razor saw; a pair of tweezers; a metal rule; some form of small plastic or metal spatula to mix up and spread the groundwork; a bowl for mixing the groundwork material (ideally rubber, for ease of cleaning, but plastic will do); and a couple of old brushes.

* * *

I appreciate that the above information is the barest minimum, but the details of the diorama and vignettes that I built for this book will give a better idea of a few of the methods and materials I have mentioned. Further on, you'll find examples of boxed dioramas, a false-perspective diorama, cutaway and framed models, and a large number of displayed pieces created by other modellers. I hope that, taken all in all, this book provides readers of any level of experience with something of interest, or may even spark an idea of devilish cunning.

# 'Ozymandias'

The idea for this diorama occurred to me when Gerry Embleton of Time Machine AG offered me this casting of a human face. Intended for one of his life-sized museum figures, it had cracked during curing and was of no use to him. It made me think of the lines from Shelley's poem 'Ozymandias', about a traveller in a far-off land who comes across the remains of a gigantic statue in the desert, all that remains of this long-forgotten king's empire: 'My name is Ozymandias, king of kings: Look on my works, ye Mighty, and despair!'. It struck me that this epitaph for a monstrous and deluded ego could equally well apply to the monomaniac who dreamed of a Thousand-Year Reich. (I must admit to some artistic licence here. In the poem, all that remained of the statue were the 'vast and trunkless legs', but I didn't feel that a pair of damn great feet had the same dramatic eye-appeal, somehow.)

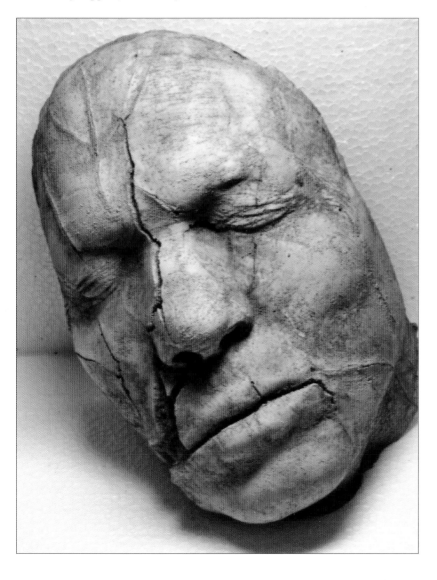

The resin mask, coated with Green Scene's 'Concrete', then weathered with MIG Productions' washes.

Starting to build up the basis for the groundwork in polystyrene foam block.

# Building the diorama

I started with the mask, which was originally cast in a yellow ochre shade of resin. The first step was to spray it with a matt grey automotive undercoat and, after this had dried overnight, I applied a generous layer of 'Concrete' from the Green Scene range of textured coatings; this dries in a patchy fashion, leaving some areas more roughly textured than others, which was the effect I was after. I left this to dry and then applied a number of washes (or filters) from MIG Productions; I used 'Tan' (P242), 'Panzer Grey' (P240), 'Brown' (P241) and 'Green' (P244). These were applied at random and in various concentrations until I was happy with the result. I then set the mask aside and started on the base.

The basis was a block of polystyrene foam measuring 20 x 12 inches and another piece the same size for the back wall. I balanced the mask on the base until I had identified the right angle. Cutting up some more pieces of poly with a hot-wire cutter, I set them either side of the mask, angling them to jut forward at the bottom so as to provide the basis for the rockface on either side of the mask, and fixed them in place with a hot-glue gun.

This done, I used Woodland Scenics' moulds to cast a number of differently shaped plaster rock sections, and built these up on the poly block base. I used a single casting over the head and then built up to that from the bottom. These rock sections can be cut and shaped to fit whatever layout you wish and, to my mind, give a more realistic appearance than carved-up polystyrene. They also take colouring better, since the paints and washes are absorbed into the plaster rather than sitting on the surface. Obviously the individual pieces won't fit exactly, like a jigsaw, and once the bulk of the work was done I then filled in the gaps with Mod-Roc plaster cloth. With the rockface in place I then used layers of Mod-Roc to build up the slope of the ground in the foreground and up to the rocks and the face. When dry, both the foreground and the rockface were given a couple of coats of the textured 'Concrete' medium (the groundwork was textured with the 'Concrete' so as to give a toothed surface on which to stick the sand.)

I had decided to build a section of ruined building on the cliff top; the vertical poly block I used for the back of the scene was 2 inches deep, and this gave me ample room. For the ruin I used (once again) my old standby, the child's building set called 'Castle Master'. The stone blocks, window apertures and broken mouldings were all cast with Eberhard Faber 'Ceramofix', which cures much faster and harder than ordinary plaster. Once the wall was built, and the various odd pieces were in place, I coloured them using a method suggested to me by Simon Ferrugia at Great North Roads: I simply sponged them with hot tea bags. You tend to find yourself frantically blowing on your fingertips a lot, but the result is worth it, with nice varying sandy-coloured hues of stone. For the ground in front of the wall I used the instant papier mâché 'Claycrete', mixing this with water to which I had already added Vallejo's Model Color Light Brown (129). I spread this along both front and back of the first row of blocks and then blended it up against the stones; while it dried I finished building the wall, using PVA white glue for 'mortar'. Once all this was done I gave the groundwork a coat of slurry made up from a mix of

The rockface built up and covered overall with Green Scene's 'Concrete'.

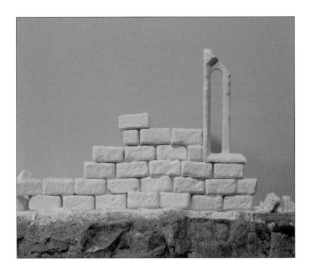

The crumbling palace walls, made from plaster blocks that I cast in moulds.

The blocks were coloured by dabbing them with hot tea bags, which gives a controllable variation in shades.

The groundwork, and parts of the rockface, covered with layers of coarse birdcage sand.

11

The added vegetation is a mixture of products and finds, from 'Silflor' Leaf Foliage and plastic plants for aquariums bought from pet shops, and my scrap box. The ground in between the wall and the rocks is coated with a thinned-out slurry of MIG Productions' 'African Earth'.

water and MIG Productions' 'African Earth' (PO38), and gave the wall a heavy dusting of the same powder, working it into all the crevices between the blocks.

The next step was the addition of vegetation. As this was supposed to be an arid desert I wanted most of the plants to look bleached and dusty, with not much green in the foliage and what there was in faded tones. Most of the vegetation came from my spares box of bits collected over the years; some was meant for use in aquariums but, as this was plastic, the very glossy finish had to be toned down with matt varnish. The mass of vegetation above the right side of the face is 'Silflor' Leaf Foliage, which is tiny leaf cover attached to a fine

The dead vines around the window embrasure are made from Spanish moss, which is available from most florists' shops.

netting backing sheet; this is very versatile, and can be teased out into any shape you need. Once it was all in place the vegetation also got a good dose of the 'African Earth' weathering powder.

Contrary to the popular perception, few deserts are made up entirely of beautifully sculpted sand dunes; the great majority of desert areas are made up of coarse sand mixed with gravelly material, and this is what I used here. Bought from a pet shop and intended for birdcages, the sand is fairly coarse and has tiny pieces of grit and shell mixed in. I coated the appropriate areas of the basework with PVA glue and then sprinkled the sand on quite liberally. Once the glue dried I blew off the excess and then sprayed it all with a clear varnish, on top of which I sprinkled another layer of sand. I repeated this until I had a good layer of sand all over the foreground and reaching up around the face, where it would have blown by the wind; I also added some to the cracks in the face and between the lips.

Some additional details had been added during the build, such as the fallen sections of ruined stonework on the rocks and the blown sand on ledges and in crevices, and the final touch on the rockface was the addition of shattered pieces of rock, made from a broken-up slate, in the gully to the left of the face. This was done to give the impression of the passage of time and weather breaking the rocks down. A final weathering was applied with MIG Productions' powders, with an additional darker streak down across the right side of the face to indicate occasional seepage from the vegetation above.

Once I have worked out where any figures are to be placed in a scene I leave the actual placing until the end, and in this case I had originally planned to place both DAK soldiers alongside the Kübelwagen, but on reflection I decided that placing one 1/48th-scale officer next to the stone face would tie the piece together and give a more striking impression of the vastness of the lost statue.

The sight-seeing Afrika Korps officer climbing up the rocks.

Shards of flaked-off rock, made from a broken-up slate, set in the coarse wind-blown sand filling the gully. In desert terrain rocks of a wide range of subtle colours can be found in quite close proximity, ranging from whites and greys through beiges, pinks and iron-browns to black.

The Tamiya 1/48th-scale Kübelwagen and Afrika Korps figures. Whatever your original plan for placing figures in a diorama, it is not always necessary to make up your mind finally until you have tried them in the finished scene to check where they look best. Placing one officer climbing up to the vast stone face ties the two contrasting elements of the model together much better than having both standing by the field car in the foreground.

The finished diorama. (Hitler actually instructed his architect Albert Speer to bear in mind the future 'noble ruin potential' of the Nazis' monumental public buildings. He never managed anything approaching this.)

# Gothic knight

I had built the Andrea kit of the knight in 15th-century fluted Germanic 'Maximilian' armour some time ago, but then it just languished at the back of a shelf. I thought it high time to give him a rather more fitting setting, and decided on making a simple vignette incorporating the figure with some sort of fortification. This straightforward subject is included here simply to demonstrate that even a single figure can be given some appealing 'context' without too much work, and while hardly enlarging the display space it takes up on your shelf.

## Building the vignette

To mount this scene I used a 'picture frame' type with a removable base. This is a useful device if you have to make repairs later, or want to 'recycle' the materials with a different scene on display – you just push up the baseboard from underneath and replace it in the frame with another, rather than having to start from scratch and build a new base.

Once the baseboard was cut to size I scored it across to give a good surface for the groundwork to adhere to. Using the horse's hooves as a template, I marked out where they would be finally be placed and drilled four holes to accept the pegs that were cast on the bottom of the hooves. Cutting four pieces of dowel, I then pushed them into the holes to ensure that the 'Claycrete' would not plug them when I was laying on the groundwork. As the scene was to be set in the winter, I mixed the 'Claycrete' with water to which I added Vallejo's Model Color 'German Grey', and also some PVA glue to prevent the groundwork drying out and cracking over time.

The 'demountable' display base. A useful variation on the most straightforward frame method is to take a strip of wooden moulding, make up the 'picture frame' to accept your diorama base on the inner lip, and then stick a horizontal piece of hardboard to the back/bottom of the frame with a fairly large hole cut in it.

The cast plaster wall blocks, textured on the visible faces with a dental burr.

The plan view of the wall section and gateway arch laid out on a grid.

The backdrop was to be a closed gateway, which seemed an apt setting for such a defiantly forbidding figure. I spread the groundwork mix across the base except for the line where I was going to build the gateway; I wanted to lay the first row of blocks on an absolutely level surface so as to ensure that the wall would be vertical. Having moulded the plaster blocks, I used a fairly large dental burr in my mini-drill and textured those faces that would be visible, but left the rest smooth to ensure a good bond between them when stuck together.

My next move was planning the actual layout of the gateway, and the easiest way to do this was to lay the blocks out on a grid so that I could move them about and make sure that the final plan would actually fit on the baseboard. Once that was done I built the walls up, using PVA glue, alternating from one side to the other as I went and finally finishing it off with the arch at the top. With the gateway finished, I turned my attention once more to the groundwork.

With the basic layer now dry, I mixed up a bit more 'Claycrete' and feathered it up to the stonework, added some ruts in front of the gate, and laid the last layer of groundwork. Once the 'Claycrete' had almost dried I removed the pegs to clear the holes for the addition of the figure later on.

Starting the gateway.

The arch in place, and four dowels inserted in the baseboard to ensure the holes for attaching the horse were kept clear.

'Claycrete' papier mâché medium, sometimes sold as 'Celluclay'.

The leaves of the gate were made from two pieces of basswood; the planking pattern was scored into them with an Olfa cutter and the score marks highlighted with black India ink. Basswood was also used for the reinforcing beams, and then the whole thing was stained with 'Weather-Rite' from Timberline Scenery in the USA. Once the stain had dried I weathered the bottom of the gate with olive green ground-up pastel chalk to give the wood the look of damp algae.

I cut the hinges from a sheet of soft lead foil, and punched out the studs from the same sheet using a $3/16$ th inch hollow punch. One bonus of using soft lead rather than Plasticard is that when you punch out bolt heads, studs, etc., the lead bows up in the centre and you wind up with nice convex heads. Once glued on with PVA, the hinges and studs were coloured using a product called 'Neolube No. 2'; this comes from Huron Industries in the States and is marketed for model railway buffs over there by Micro-Mark. It is a mix of graphite and IPA (isopropyl alcohol) and when applied to metal surfaces it gives a satin finish very close to that of clean iron. It is easily applied with a brush and dries almost instantly; I use it a lot for various dark metal finishes, particularly on white metal (it's excellent if you want a realistic parkerized finish on World War II weapons).

I made up a short section of portcullis to show above the gate, using the lead grid that is – was? – used to form the cells in automobile batteries. (I got several of these years ago from a chap who used to recondition batteries, but I suppose they may be a thing of the past by now.) I cut the grid to give the pattern of iron bars I needed, then coated it first with 'Rustall' before adding contrasting patches of MIG Productions' 'Light Rust' weathering powder. The same method was used to make the bars in the arrow-slit beside the gateway. The last touch to the gateway was to carefully line the tops of the hinges and beams on the gate with PVA glue, using a toothpick, and then to sprinkle Woodland Scenics' snow powder onto the glue.

With the gateway and gates up it was time to add some colour. Since I wanted the colouring in this vignette to have a colder feel I gave the stonework several washes of heavily thinned out 'Stone Grey' from the Woodland Scenics' 'Earth Colour' set, ran thinned-out black paint into the cracks between the blocks, and then airbrushed a light coat of satin varnish over the whole thing. It was finished off by carefully filling some of the crevices with snow powder. The bare earth groundwork in front of the gate was washed over with satin varnish to give it a muddy look and then lightly sprinkled with snow. Either side of the track was covered with a grass matting called 'Savannah Dry Turf' from Silflor; this has clumps of grass interspersed with bare patches of earth, and comes in four seasonal varieties. I used the 'Spring' tone, and then dulled down the grass colouring by airbrushing a light mist of tan paint over it to give it a dead and sere look. I applied a light sprinkling of snow over all the grass areas, and added a dead, leafless bush made from copper wire.

Finally, I dripped superglue into the four holes left in the groundwork and put the knight in place. Now my man of iron had a suitably forbidding setting – 'They shall not pass . . .'.

The groundwork, of 'Celluclay' mixed with suitable colouring, has been laid on and the four dowel plugs removed.

RIGHT The basswood gates under construction.

LEFT The lead grid material from old automotive batteries that I use to make rusty iron bar work.

The portcullis and the grille on the slit window to the left of the archway in place.

'Winter Sunlight'.

# 'Safari Rally 1971'

In about 1960 I gave up modelling as a hobby and spent some ten years as an amateur rally driver, tearing around the UK and Continental Europe 'frightening the horses and startling the ladies'. I can assure you that the following vignette brings back some memories – like the sound of your suspension giving way, or the strange feeling of looking at the world from a wholly new perspective as your car settles into the scenery on its roof . . . The car in this case is a Datsun 240Z, the type that won the East African Safari Rally in 1971. The model itself is an old 1/24th-scale Hasegawa kit, built pretty much straight from the box except for additional detailing inside. It is included here to demonstrate the 'added visual value' that can be given to a single vehicle model by setting it in groundwork that conveys its context.

## Building the vignette

The base is, as usual, a block of polystyrene, but this time I didn't give it an overall coating of 'Claycrete'. Instead, I roughly drew out the area of the track and then cut two pieces of Silflor 'Savannah' grass matting, and glued them down with Woodland Scenics' cement. Once the glue had dried completely I cut out the holes where I was going the place the rocky outcrops – this ensures that the rocks 'grow out of' the groundwork rather than sitting on top.

The next step was moulding the flattish rock on which the large outcrop would rest together with its surrounding features, and then finally the large rock itself and the smaller rocks to go in the grass and the track. I cast all these, in a variety of Woodland Scenics' rubber moulds, from Eberhard Faber 'Ceramofix' casting material; this is very tough and can be pulled out of the mould within about half an hour, ready for painting.

The track came next, for which I used Woodland Scenics' 'Hydrocal' lightweight plaster – I wanted a material that would take a bit longer drying so that I could work the surface into ruts and ridges, as well as pressing in a couple of rocks. I mixed up the 'Hydrocal' with water to which I had previously added burnt sienna powder paint.

The main rock outcrop placed on the polystyrene base and the rough outline of the track traced out.

The strips of grass matting have been glued down, the track made up with 'Hydrocal' lightweight plaster, and the various rocks in place

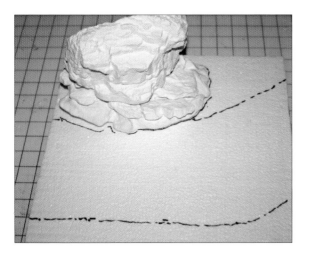

With the basics complete, I then airbrushed the rocks with a thinned-down solution of 'African Earth' weathering powder (MIG Productions PO38), and also brushed some undiluted powder into the grasses, where the dust raised by passing cars would have blown it. I also spread the powder on the track, once again as a covering of dust.

The vegetation used was a mixture of 'sea foam' to represent sun-bleached bush, and some odd pieces with little yellow tufts from my spares box. The dead sapling on the rockface is just wire and plaster, with some herbs for the fallen leaves.

## The car

When the Datsun kit had been built and detailed it was airbrushed with Tamiya Red gloss and Black matt paints. I must add here that Iwata has brought out an accessory to its airbrush range that I found extremely useful. This is an air control valve that you screw in between the air line and the airbrush, enabling you to adjust the airflow (the product reference is the K250 MAC valve).

Make your rocks and boulders 'grow out of' the ground. Nothing looks worse than having them apparently dropped on from above, like the rubber boulders at the Burbank studios fondly remembered from early series of a certain Hollywood space-opera.

The finished groundwork and the added vegetation, with a good covering of dust added to the rocks and track.

A detail of some of the vegetation. I have no idea what type of African plant has yellow tufts, and I'm not deranged enough to spend time finding out, but I'm prepared to bet there is a weed that does – what matters is that it *looks* African.

The 240Z under construction. Although little of the interior would be visible, like any true modeller I couldn't resist adding details. The seat harnesses can just about be seen through the windscreen, together with the dust that gets into the cars in copious quantities.

The padding around the roll bar was made with lengths of yellow plastic tubing, and the tape is very narrow black masking tape as used on printed circuit boards.

Once the car was painted and the decals applied, I then vandalized the suspension, tore up the tyre, and coated the whole thing with 'African Earth' let down with thinners to give the vehicle a good covering of dust. The heavier splashes of mud were a thicker mix, flicked on with an old toothbrush. (Marcus Nicholls did a similar treatment to a rally car in *Tamiya Model Magazine International* Special Issue 99, with a very good picture spread of each stage.) And if any of you think the weathering on this model is overdone, I promise you that it's not.

The spare wheels are secured in the boot with scratch-built bungees made from Verlinden rubber piping, with the hooks made from a sheet of brass-etch buckles and straps. The oilcan is from Plus Models.

The title of this piece is '*@#*!! – that sounds expensive!'

The sad-looking 240Z in place, from various viewpoints.

# Bases and cases

Many companies supply bases, cases or both, and contact details for some of these will be found in the Appendix. In this section I have simply illustrated a very few of the ways of mounting figures and other models.

Nicely figured, stained and polished wooden bases lend themselves to almost any type of individual figure or small-scale model. These particular ones are made by Stan Britnell (contact details in the Appendix).

Stan's bases, plus a case bought some years ago from an Italian company, DOC Models. The nice thing about the latter is that it is mostly glass, with very slender brass rods supporting the top, so it provides a good uninterrupted all-round view of your model.

If you want to keep the cost down, keep your eyes open for recycling opportunities. The box in the foreground is one in which I received a fairly potent bottle of something one Christmas; its plastic front slides right out, as seen here. The other, seen from the rear, is a cheap glass-fronted box from a discount store; it can be opened in the same way, and as you can see it has fittings for hanging on a wall either upright or sideways. These sorts of boxes can be sandpapered or painted and made into perfectly good display cases for very little cost.

Charles Davis adopted a novel approach to displaying these Napoleonic figures. The domed clock had given up the ghost, so he gave it a second lease of life by creating this original display unit.

This is a very adaptable case that I've had for a long time. It will accept some fairly large dioramas – note the 1/35th-scale figure inside, to give an idea of scale.

Another dome display, this time a beautifully painted fairy by Geoffrey Illsley.

Although not yet cased, this Napoleonic trumpeter figure painted by Charles Davis is photographed to show the advantages of having a mirror-backed display case when there is much fine detail on the back of a model.

Two of the excellent weapons – a Bren light machine gun and an MG42 – that I bought from Present Arms, seen on the base of a display case. These wonderful quarter-scale kits, cast in white metal to the highest degree of accuracy and detail, cry out for careful display, especially as they are in a scale that may be very different from those of other models on your shelves, from which they need to be set apart visually.

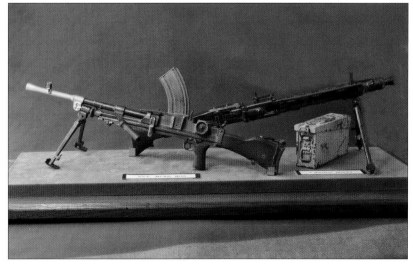

Quarter-scale Short Magazine Lee Enfield .303in rifle and M1 Garand .30cal semi-automatic rifle, mounted on basswood covered with green baize, to be placed at the back of the case.

The assembled weapons display.

# Light boxes

Two or three years ago I was asked by Time Machine AG to build a scene that Gerry Embleton had designed for display in a watch and clock museum in Switzerland. Apparently, during the 19th century farmers in the alpine valleys who were snowbound for most of the winter turned to repairing clocks and watches, and this diorama was to depict an old craftsman at his workbench.

Starting work on constructing the workshop. Note that the 'room' is set at angle to the outer box. All the wooden elements in the scene, including the floor and walls, were made with varying gauges of basswood.

Even in the 19th century the Swiss had a fairly efficient system of double-glazing; this shows the outer casement in place.

The inner casement. The brass sockets for the swing-bar are made from scrap brass etching, and the knob is from my scrap box. Note the small icicles at the top left.

At this stage you can obviously see the shadows thrown by the glazing bars of the window on the snow scene outside, but once the lighting for the window is in place these will disappear. This is one of the most important things to remember when building a light box: you must ensure that no shadows are thrown on the background scenery – a shadow of a figure or an object cast inside an enclosed room scene is not a problem, but a shadow cast on exterior landscape looks terrible.

The room taking shape. The 'ceiling' beams are fixed the inner side of the outer box, which I stained and scored to represent the plank flooring of the room above. Note that the room's left-hand wall is not yet in place.

The workbench in place by the window, with a longcase clock standing by the wall.

Checking the size of the 'mask' for the front of the box.

Scratch-building the stove. The main body is plastic piping, with a Plasticard door added. The 'cast-iron' decoration is in fact cheap costume jewellery, which easily bent to shape for attachment with superglue.

The finished stove in place. Note the ash pan, a fairly essential piece of equipment when a stove is installed on a nice dry wooden floor.

Detail shot of the oil lamp and some of the tools on the workbench. I used a turned wooden bead for the lamp base and a piece of plastic rod turned on a small lathe to make the glass chimney; the brass collar and knob for the wick are of scrap etch brass.

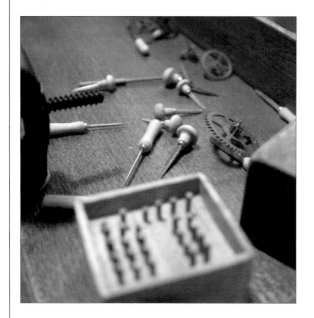

A better shot of the miniature tools, beautifully made for me by Gavin Haslup.

Gavin also made this adjustable stool, which actually works.

Looking into the completed workroom, you can see the two separate light sources: one from the passageway beyond the open door, and the other – a cold wintry light – coming through the window. The splendid figure of the old man was scratch-built by Gillian Roberts. The clock is made from thin basswood stained with dark oak; I scanned the face from a book on antiques, printed it to the size I needed and gave a 3D effect to the hands by adding a faint pencil 'shadow' under them. (Photo: Time Machine AG)

How the finished scene was finally mounted in the museum. The superb lighting effects were created by a stage lighting specialist, but the basic principles can be grasped by any modeller who creates this kind of enclosed scene. This view also emphasizes the obvious fact that a masked frontal viewpoint does not mean that any less care can be taken over the interior side surfaces, whatever scale you are working in. (Photo: Time Machine AG; lighting by Mati AG, Zurich)

# Shep Paine

Shep Paine is known worldwide for building stunning dioramas and 'shadow boxes', as well as for his skills as a sculptor of masters for white-metal figures over some 30 years. His two books *How to Build Dioramas* and *Modeling Tanks and Military Vehicles*, published by Kalmbach Publishing in the States during the 1980s, must be two of the most popular books on the subject ever written (they certainly started me off on gravitating from just building a model to creating a scene for it). His light boxes and dioramas have been eagerly sought by artists and collectors alike, and his work is to be found in some of America's most prestigious collections, including the Museum of Science and Industry in Chicago and the Forbes Gallery in New York.

RIGHT Shep's incredibly detailed model 'The Night Watch', recreating Rembrandt's famous painting of 1642.

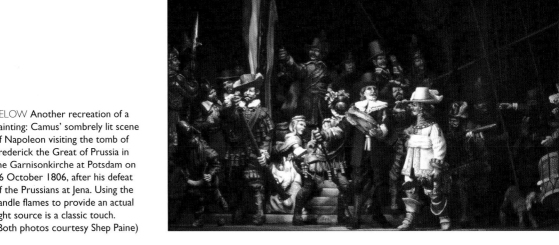

BELOW Another recreation of a painting: Camus' sombrely lit scene of Napoleon visiting the tomb of Frederick the Great of Prussia in the Garnisonkirche at Potsdam on 26 October 1806, after his defeat of the Prussians at Jena. Using the candle flames to provide an actual light source is a classic touch. (Both photos courtesy Shep Paine)

# Ernie Mirfin

Although Ernie now concentrates on painting rather than modelling, in the past he built some striking 'light boxes' (a branch of modelling, by the way, that he feels is sadly neglected these days). I have never forgotten seeing his 'Yesterday's Comrades' many years ago at EuroMilitaire, and I am grateful to him for permission to illustrate it here.

A view of the inner box containing the model, showing the set-up of the lighting. Obviously, since all this is never seen you don't have to create a masterpiece of carpentry in here.

A slightly closer shot, showing the Vietnam War veteran lost in his memories as he pauses at the Memorial Wall in Washington, DC, on his way home from work on a summer evening.

LEFT The light box with the front frame and mask in place.

BELOW The magic of Ernie's design: turn the lights on, and the Memorial Wall suddenly becomes transparent, revealing ghostly figures in battledress. Note the way that Ernie has arranged the veteran's pose so that his raised hand is nearly mirrored by the hand of the nearest figure seen 'behind' the wall. The ghostly effect was achieved by airbrushing transparent plastic sheet with a thinned solution of black paint, which looks opaque until the light is turned on, whereupon the figures of the 'ghosts' become visible. It took Ernie a month to work out how to reproduce the enormous list of names that adorn the wall, and about a week to put them in place.

'The Death of Nelson' – Ernie's depiction of this famous moment is based upon a well-known painting. Unfortunately it was impossible to get good photos of this model once the front cover and glass were in place – the reflection on the glass rendered the detail almost invisible. Here we see the set of the inner box with two spotlights high up at either side, and the electric cable feeding in through the back under the ship's 'deck'.

Here the scene is illuminated by the overhead lantern and the lantern at Nelson's feet.

Close-up of the scene illuminated; note the third lantern held by the figure standing beyond the sailor kneeling at left. (All photos courtesy Ernie Mirfin)

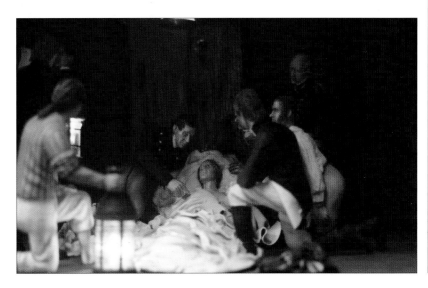

39

# Framed displays

Sideview of a frame for a model by Charles Davis, showing additional depth added to the original frame using thin plywood.

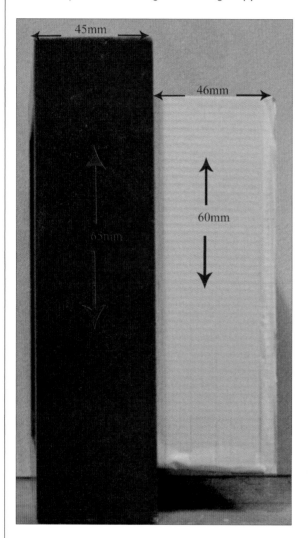

In this view of the model of the Napoleonic Gendarme you can see the extra depth inside the frame, allowing Charles to incorporate a semi-round tree with Woodland Scenics' scatter for foliage, and a painted backdrop.

A framed pair of 'flats' in the author's collection – flats obviously lend themselves to this kind of display particularly well. The two knights are mounted on green velvet; the frame is actually glassed over, but this doesn't show in the photo.

A clever presentation of a 'flat' between two separate layers of glass in a light wooden frame, made by Gavin Haslup.

Detail: the trees nearest the viewer are painted on the reverse of the first layer of glass. Behind the figure a second layer of glass is also painted on its reverse face with more trees; finally the backdrop, painted with the hills and distant trees, is added. This model is now owned by Lynn Sangster, to whom I am grateful for permission to photograph it.

# False perspective

These photos show 'behind-the-scenes' and 'viewer's perspective' (head-on) views of a large false-perspective diorama that I built for Time Machine AG displays in the Lake Dwelling Museum at Unteruhldingen on the shores of Lake Constance in Switzerland. Obviously, this 'behind-the-scenes' shot shows it still under construction, but the central part is finished and the steps taken to construct the model can be explained. (Photos courtesy Time Machine AG)

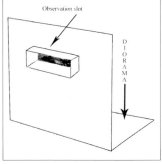

The viewers' vision was to be tightly controlled by a slot in the front face board with a boxed surround on the outside (see white arrow '1' in the behind-the-scenes photo). This boxing of the slot is necessary to reinforce the viewers' illusion of distance. If they could get their faces right up to the viewing slot, then by looking up and to either side they would be able to see where the painted backdrop scenery joined the roof and sides of the outer box. This backdrop was fastened to the long curved strip across the baseboard, visible behind the diorama in both photos, and the lake was created in the gap between that and the shore. As it is, the box holds viewers far enough back that they can only see what we want them to see.

## Making the baseboard

I began by cutting irregular shapes of sandwich board, each layer being shallower from front to back than the one below it, so that when they were glued down on the baseboard they formed overlapped steps, with the irregularly-cut edges towards the back of the scene. Each of these progressive 'drops' (from foreground ledge at white arrow 2, to blue arrows 3, 4 and 5) would create the illusion of 'dead ground', beyond which the modelling would be done in progressively smaller scales.

A rather deeper ledge of groundwork was built up against the front board of the base; then the large trees on the left of the head-on picture were secured into this ledge. These trees had been scratch-built previously from wire, plaster and foliage; the largest piece of foliage, which showed closest to the viewing slot, was made from brass photo-etch from Scale Link and the remainder from Woodland Scenics' scatter and clump foliage. I brought the brass-etch foliage into view at the left and top edges of the viewing slot, so as to give the impression of standing in the edge of a hilltop wood looking out and down to the village on the lake shore.

Once the foreground trees were in place I covered their bases and the ledge with different grasses, flock groundwork, leaf litter, and the large logs and branches that can be see in the head-on view (these were made from wire armatures with a plaster coating). The foreground ledge had been made with a step in it, so that I could give the impression that the path where the young lad was dragging a log away was lying a bit lower than the area where the woodsman was working (again, see head-on view).

With the foreground complete with the exception of the figures, I worked my way towards the back of the scene, gradually building up the groundwork on each succeeding 'step' of the sandwich board. I made the ground cover less and less coarse as I went, so that not only trees, shrubs and hedges but even the grass got smaller and smaller 'in the distance'. The hedges surrounding the furthest fields

The perspective effect was enhanced by diminishing the size of the figures. Those in the very foreground were between 5 and 6 inches tall; although not visible here, there was also a 1/35th-scale figure appearing up the hill to the right; the one on the track just visible to the left of the woodcutter's head (yellow arrow) is a small-scale Preiser railway layout figure, and those between the forest and the land being cleared for crops in the far right distance (yellow arrow) are about the smallest Preiser figures you can get. The finished model even had some people on the beach to the right of the village, but as these were represented by tiny lengths of bristle cut from an old brush I'm afraid they don't show in these pictures. The two foreground figures were scratch-built by Gillian Robinson, who also made the clothing and the axe, working from information provided by the museum staff. (She also made a family of wild pigs, out of shot to the left amongst the trees.)

were simply lengths of string soaked in PVA glue and rolled in green scatter. By comparison with the large trees in the foreground, the forest in the distance on the right-hand side by the 'lake shore' was Woodland Scenics' clump foliage stuck directly to the baseboard. The village on the lake shore was made from small cubes of wood with one side cut to a pitch to suggest the roofs, and then surrounded by a long, curved length of very thin veneer painted to resemble a stockade – the whole thing was about 6 inches long and 2 inches deep. The various fields were coated with differing shades of scatter, not representing any particular crop but giving a nice patchwork effect to the landscape.

As can be seen in the behind-the-scenes photo, the drops in depth between the layers of sandwich board are very shallow, but it is not necessary to make these dramatic to get the desired effect of depth and distance. I only needed to make the path from the foreground to the village markedly narrower as it crossed and reappeared behind each ridge of the terrain in order to create – when viewed from the front – the impression of looking out from a hilltop over a distance of several kilometres.

Once all the scenery was completed, the whole diorama was fitted inside a large outer casing and set in the wall of a room, with the viewing slot at adult's eye level and a small ramp for children. The lighting shone through diffusers above to give the scene the appearance of natural daylight. Sadly, although this piece has been installed at the museum for some time now I've never actually seen it in its final form with the backdrop scenery and lighting in place – my work had finished before that point and I had to return to England.

# Cutaway models

While cutaway models don't appear in modelling competitions very often, I thought it might be useful to include a brief section on this type of scene, since a number of military scenarios do lend themselves to this kind of treatment. The most obvious application would be some kind of 'visual story' contrasting what was happening on either side of the door connecting two rooms, or 'upstairs and downstairs' (various scenarios, both poignant and humorous, suggest themselves), but this approach would also suit pillboxes, bunkers and even siege-mines. Some time ago Time Machine AG commissioned me to make a few of these cutaways for display in a museum at Vaduz, Liechtenstein. These three were to be shown in a section devoted to methods of heating formerly used on the Continent, from roughly Roman times up to the 1800s.

This is a model of a big stove, clad with ceramic tiles, set in a late 19th-century rural house; such stoves were integrated with a cooking range and were accessible from two rooms, providing the main heating for the house. (This arrangement could be found right across Central Europe and into Russia from at least the 17th century onwards, and military memoirs mention soldiers sleeping crowded around and even on top of the tiled stoves in winter.)

The cutaway walls of the living room were made up from polystyrene sheet, cut raggedly at the top. These were then clad with very heavy white cartridge paper and painted with acrylic matt white. I painted the central cross-section of the walls a distinctly darker colour so as to contrast with the light outer faces. The planking for the floor is made up from short lengths of basswood, stained with an aging fluid called 'Weather-It' which is obtainable from Micro-Mark in the States. The door and doorframe were also made from basswood, finished with a dark oak stain, and I left the door standing ajar so as to make a visual connection with the kitchen on the other side of the wall. I built the carcass of the stove from stout cardboard and then clad it in Plasticard, into which I engraved the outlines of the tiles.

ABOVE This is the kitchen that connects with the living room. On this side of the polystyrene sheet wall I used a very heavily textured artist's watercolour paper that looked like rough plaster when it had been painted and slightly soot-stained. The oven was again made using a cardboard skeleton skinned with Plasticard; it and all the metal ash-doors in the model were treated in the same way, with the Plasticard painted matt black and then heavily worked over with graphite for a metallic sheen.

ABOVE A detailed shot of one of the cooker's doors, showing the metallic sheen you can achieve by rubbing graphite over matt black paint. The knobs are made by holding a length of Plastirod near a flame – as the rod heats up it rolls away from the flame and forms a neat knob; just cut it off and cement it to your model.

RIGHT Cutaway of a chamber in a small Roman domestic bathhouse, showing how the rooms were heated using an under-floor hypocaust. The walls are built in the same way as before but the outer wall, on the left, had to have an inner cavity added to illustrate the way that the heat from the hypocaust was carried up through flues in the wall to heat the rooms. For this I used lengths of rectangular 'Plastruct', cutting them at an ever-increasing angle as they were exposed higher and higher up the wall. The short brick pillars supporting the bathroom floor were once again made from 'Balsafoam'. (All photos by kind permission of Frau U. Mayr, Landesmuseum, Vaduz)

ABOVE Through the open door you can see the figure of a man warming his hands at the stove in the living room while his wife cooks in the kitchen; the wall has now been soot-stained. Both these figures were made for me by Gavin Haslup.

ABOVE This is a cutaway of a Roman pottery kiln. The dome shape was made by coating with plaster a plastic bowl in which a well-known company sold a small Christmas pudding. The cutaway section of the brick interior is carved from 'Balsafoam', indented with the courses between the bricks and painted with acrylic paints. The dishes to be fired are stacked on a shelf above the furnace chamber. The same basic principles of construction would apply equally well to, say, a bunker in Normandy or on the Siegfried Line.

# Gallery

## Geoffrey Illsley

The following pages feature models of a remarkably wide range of subjects made by Geoffrey Illsley, chief judge for the EuroMilitaire show (sadly, this illustrious position prevents him from entering the competitions any more). These pictures clearly show how his scratch-building abilities, meticulous attention to detail, painting skills and masterly use of the airbrush have brought him many gold medals and 'best of show' awards over the years.

Busts, of a 'Blood Warrior' and the Ancient Egyptian Queen Nefertari.

TOP 'The Apache'.
ABOVE The rattlesnake lurking in the base groundwork exemplifies the kind of imaginative detail that can give a delightful 'lift' to the presentation of a single figure.

LEFT Tazio Nuvolari, a legend amongst pre-war racing drivers of both cars and motorcycles (for one motorbike race he had himself tied to the machine, since he had broken both his legs in a recent crash; he won the race). The presentation of the 'caption' on a signboard 'inside' the vignette is a neat solution that avoids having to make a base deep enough for a plaque carrying so much information.

The harvest's in ... A bobby talks with two young sightseers at Mays Farm, Berwick, Sussex, on 12 August 1940, when Uffz Zaunbrecher of 2/JG 2 force-landed his Bf109E-1 'red 14' after being damaged by P/O McClintock of 615 Sqn RAF. Such groundwork as the convincing torn-up earth track of a belly-landing demands patient skill.

'Little Miss Mischief' of the 325th Sqn, 95th Bomb Group, 8th USAAF, on a hard-standing with tarred seams. This Flying Fortress was a perfect example of 'cut and shut' rebuilding of damaged aircraft: the rear fuselage and the two starboard engine cowlings came from one B-17, and the rest of the 'plane from another.

LEFT This private in the 1st (Petrograd) Women's Death Battalion, Russia, 1917, displays the nice touch of an over-sized man's uniform and boots. The simple groundwork matches the terrain and season for the Kerenski summer offensive in which the unit was almost wiped out.

RIGHT 'Stitching the Standard'. Geoffrey's model is taken from a painting by the Victorian artist Blair Leighton. Leighton's composition could hardly be bettered; posing the lady on the battlements provides pleasing contrasts between her femininity and the harsh stonework, and between the colours of the standard and her pale costume and the stone-grey.

'Readiness'. This diorama, centred on the legless fighter ace Sqn Ldr Douglas Bader's Hurricane of No. 242 Sqn at RAF Coltishall, won the special Battle of Britain Museum Trophy awarded at EuroMilitaire in September 1990, the 50th anniversary of the battle.

BELOW Detail from 'Readiness': the legless ace Douglas Bader standing by his Hurricane.

LEFT Geoffrey was not too happy with the instrument panel or seat for the Hurricane provided by the kit, so he meticulously scratch-built replacements – despite the fact that they would be almost invisible in the finished model.

ABOVE & RIGHT A 1/72nd-scale Heller kit of an Arado Ar196A-3 floatplane of Bordflieger 196, heavily rebuilt by Geoffrey. The launch catapult and railings are brass etch from White Ensign. On the navigator's table inside the cockpit are a map of the Baltic and a pair of dividers (we repeat – this is a 1/72nd-scale kit).

'The Pursuit'. an extraordinarily well animated vignette, in which the replication of animal fur and hide is particularly well realized.

# Chris Grove

Chris spent some 30 years in the Queen's Regiment, serving in Germany, Hong Kong and the UK. During his time with 'Kirke's Lambs' he started modelling these 'Braille scale' kits, and has kept at it ever since. Unlike most of the displays pictured in this book, these are included as an example of miniaturist skills that would be visually overwhelmed by any but the simplest bases.

ABOVE US Reo 2½-ton truck M35A2, built from the CMSC 1/76th-scale kit.

LEFT British Saladin armoured car of 4th Royal Tank Regiment, which served in Borneo, 1964, during the Indonesian Confrontation.

BELOW LEFT AMX13 M52 of the French 4th Dragoons, c.1973. Built from the Heller 1/72nd-scale kit, it has quite a few improved details including tracks from the Esci Hetzer.

BOTTOM LEFT Scratch-built Mk 11 Land Rover (also known as the Series III), to 1/76th scale. It is shown as one serving in Germany in 1982.

A VAB armoured personnel carrier of the French Foreign Legion's 2nd Foreign Infantry Regiment, serving in Operation *Daguet* during the First Gulf War, 1991. It was built from the Heller 1/72nd-scale kit with a multitude of photo-etch additions.

# Roy Hunt

Roy Hunt, whose death at the shockingly early age of 49 in July 2008 was a great loss not only to his family and friends but also to the modelling world, was a master figure-modeller. Always willing to share his knowledge with anyone who was interested, he was a man of unfailing good humour, and it was always a pleasure to be in his company. I am proud to be able to include some examples of Roy's work in this book, thanks to Mrs Pat Hunt and Roy's good friend Dave Maddox.

BELOW LEFT 'The Brigand' – a spirited recreation of one of Gerry Embleton's paintings for Osprey Men-at-Arms 58, *The Landsknechts*.

BELOW CENTRE An immaculately painted Japanese warrior, Koboyakawa Takanage.

BELOW RIGHT A beautifully painted banner in Roy's vignette from the battle of Villalar, 21 April 1521, when the Emperor Charles V defeated the Comuneros.

BELOW 'God's Children'. A masterly piece, encompassing the pain and bewilderment of Hiroshima in an area of a couple of square inches. This emphasises the fact that you don't have to create a large model to evoke a powerful atmosphere. (All photos courtesy Mrs Pat Hunt)

# Mike Taylor

Mike is a self-taught artist and designer who began painting 'flats' in the 1980s and subsequently turned to designing them. Several sets of his figures have been produced worldwide, and the National Tin Figure Museum at Ommen in the Netherlands displays many of them. Following several 'best of show' awards in both the USA and UK, Mike was made a 'World Master' in 1998, and these few examples of his work show why. The options for displaying 'flats' are naturally limited; these jewel-like little masterpieces of painting need an absolutely undistracting background.

BELOW Mike is an enthusiast for the Tenniel illustrations in *Alice in Wonderland* and *Alice Through the Looking-Glass*. These are the Dodo, the Lion and the Lobster; Alice, the Gryphon and the Mad Hatter; and the King and Queen of Hearts.

RIGHT Mike is also well known for his flats depicting Ancient Egyptian subjects; this is a hunting scene with a reed boat in the marshes of the Nile.

BELOW Before-and-after photos of one of Mike's figures based on the Flower Fairies pictures, in this case 'Hemp'.

RIGHT 'Girl on a Fish' – it took Mike a week's work before he was satisfied with the fish's eye … The inset miniature shows how the piece is displayed in its frame.

# Shep Paine

The Chicago modeller Shep Paine is internationally renowned not only for his superb 'light boxes'; his more conventionally displayed dioramas, and his books, have inspired thousands of modellers over the years to strive for greater realism.

In Shep's urban diorama 'The Road to Damascus', Israeli troops examine a knocked-out Syrian T-62 during the 1973 Yom Kippur War. In the background a Super Sherman is being recovered on an armoured M26 'Dragon Wagon.. Such dioramas need careful research, rather than simply suggesting 'generic' buildings; here the specifics of a modern Middle Eastern town – concrete buildings pocked with gunfire, and masses of trailing telephone wire – add greatly to the effect

LEFT In a completely different style, the superbly animated 'A Whiff of Grapeshot' gives a grim depiction of the results of short-range artillery fire on a charge by Napoleonic cavalry. Note Shep's use of fibres to represent both the horses' tails and the maned crests of the Cuirassiers' helmets.

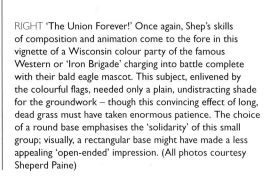

RIGHT 'The Union Forever!' Once again, Shep's skills of composition and animation come to the fore in this vignette of a Wisconsin colour party of the famous Western or 'Iron Brigade' charging into battle complete with their bald eagle mascot. This subject, enlivened by the colourful flags, needed only a plain, undistracting shade for the groundwork – though this convincing effect of long, dead grass must have taken enormous patience. The choice of a round base emphasises the 'solidarity' of this small group; visually, a rectangular base might have made a less appealing 'open-ended' impression. (All photos courtesy Sheperd Paine)

# David Irving-James

Although he has only been modelling for two or three years, David's 30 years in the British Army, starting as a boy soldier at the age of 15, have left him with a vast amount of personal knowledge of military dress, equipment and vehicles. His favourite periods of history to model are World War II and the Vietnam War. He freely admits that he has more to learn about modelling, but his dioramas have already won awards and are proof that age is no bar to starting off in our hobby. These photos show two dioramas of scenes from the North-West Europe campaigns of 1944–45.

'The Casualty Clearing Station'. Ambulances backing up to the entrance to the operating theatre set up in an outbuilding.

Detail from David's clearing station diorama: in a sombre little group isolated in the midst of the bustle, a chaplain gives the last rites to a soldier who made it no further than triage.

LEFT & BELOW 'The Plan of Battle' – Gen Eisenhower visits Montgomery's forward headquarters in the field. The sea of khaki presented by this realistically crowded scene is broken up here and there by well-placed touches of colour, such as the 'Redcap', a staff officer's scarlet cap band, and the occasional regimentally-coloured beret and field service cap.

## *ModelX* Magazine

My thanks are due to Mike Rinaldi, the editor of this US publication, for contacting on my behalf the five modellers whose work appears in these pages – and to Johan Fohlin, Michael Fichtenmayer, Antonio Martin Tello, Bryan Krueger and Jaume Ortiz for permission to reproduce these photos of their work (all courtesy of the individual modellers and *ModelX* magazine).

RIGHT 'Kurland Kessel'. SS-Frw PzGren Regt 24 'Danmark' in the Second Battle of Kurland, October 1944. Johan Fohlin's vignette, using 1/35th-scale Dragon figures with Hornet heads and scratch-built details, is displayed on a base shaped to create the realistic visual effect of infantrymen taking cover behind a fold in sloping ground.

'Kampfgruppe Saalbach'. Another 'Nordland' Division subject, featuring the armoured recce battalion in Latvia, July 1944. The half-track is a combination of the 1/35th-scale Dragon SdKfz 250/1 and Tamiya SdKfz 250/9 kits, with Royal Models PE detail sets, and figures from Alpine Miniatures and Dragon with resin heads and new details added. Again, his base – incorporating a slight slope and just enough realistic greenery – lends the vignette more eye-appeal than a single level.

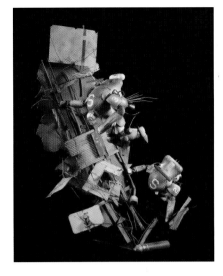

FAR LEFT 'The Copper Man'. Fichtenmayer's essentially scratch-built figure has the air of something dreamt up by Jules Verne – maybe a Victorian SEAL?

LEFT Fichtenmayer's science-fiction scene 'Patrol in the Debris Field' employs 1/20th-scale Nitto Maschinen Krieger 'Fireball SG' suits with scratch-built details, base structure and wreckage. When presented against the black background a striking effect is achieved of the spaceship crew and wreckage floating free of gravity.

RIGHT 'KV-X2 to Victory'. Michael Fichtenmayer's imaginative 'robot walker' in 1/35th scale is scratch-built using the Trumpeter KV-2 turret. Note the nice finish on the edge of the scratch-built base, whose sloped profile gives a dramatic viewing angle from the front, looking upwards at the lumbering steel monster on the skyline.

FAR LEFT & LEFT Two views of Bryan Krueger's 'Heavy Super Armored Fighting Suit', which began as a 1/20th-scale Maschinen Krieger kit from Nitto that Bryan converted by extensive scratch-building. The Nitto MaK kits are a Japanese science-fiction series first popular in the 1990s and now enjoying something of a resurgence. The original designs were created by Kow Yokoyama back in 1985 and popularized by *Hobby Japan* magazine; kits followed shortly afterwards, and are now sought after by collectors. New releases are due from Hasegawa, Wave and Nitto.

ABOVE Jaume Ortiz's 54mm Andrea Miniatures Seaforth Highlander, painted with acrylics and set on a scratch-built base. This is a perfect example of the simplest approach to displaying a single figure, on a modest but skilfully finished piece of groundwork that is absolutely in sympathy with the subject (the Seaforths' 1st Battalion served in the Sudan in 1898) without drawing the eye away from the impressive painting of the figure.

As simple in its way, and as immediately striking, is Antonio Martin Tello's 'In God We Trust'. This employs the 1/35th-scale Italeri M24 Chaffee with the Formations resin conversion set, figures from Alpine Miniatures and Yosci, and church ruins from the Spanish company Escenart. Antonio has skilfully maintained a harmoniously chilly look throughout this model. The grey stone of the towering ruin set off by the muted fragments of stained glass, the muffled-up figures of the tank crew and his use of a grey backdrop all combine to create a convincingly wintery feel.

# John Burnham

After some 22 years in the Royal Navy, during part of which time John served on HMS *Ark Royal*, it was unsurprising that when he took up modelling his main subject would be ships. He enjoys both enhancing Airfix ship kits and scratch-building those for which there is no kit. Displaying 'waterline' ship models naturally demands sea-effect bases, and these take more care – and repay more thought – than might at first appear.

John makes his bases from styrene sheet, DAS modelling clay and moulded wooden beading. Depending on the model, he starts by cutting the hull of the ship for a waterline display. The styrene sheet is cut to the appropriate size and the thickness is determined by the weight of the model or diorama, generally 2mm to 3mm. He then glues ready-cut 3.2mm x 4mm strips of styrene on top around the outer edges of the base to make a shallow 'tray'; by varying the number of strips attached in this way John has a choice as to how deep he makes the 'sea'. Once the strips are dry he scores the base to give a firm 'tooth' for the DAS clay to grip.

HMS *Ark Royal*, scratch-built to 1/600th scale.

DAS is a water-based putty that is available in white or terracotta colours. John takes a portion and rolls it out with a rolling-pin, just like a piece of pastry, preventing the DAS from sticking by dusting the rolling-pin with talcum powder first. He rolls it out to a thickness just a bit deeper than the border of the base, then places it and rolls it level to the top edges, removing any excess putty with a knife. Once this is done, he gently presses the model into the putty in the desired position. At this stage, before the putty sets, it can be moulded to the required sea effect. Any round or curved object will do for this – John normally uses the handle of a small screwdriver. To create the foam of the bow wave and wake he dabbles the bristles of an old toothbrush into the putty. Once this is done, he carefully removes the model from the putty bed and sets the base aside to dry. The length of time the DAS takes to cure depends on the amount used; as it dries it turns from a light grey colour to white (you may find that as the putty dries out it shrinks around the edges and small cracks appear, but these are easily repaired with a bit more putty). Once the DAS is thoroughly dry the whole surface can be sealed with PVA glue diluted with water.

When the sealant layer is completely dry it can be painted in whatever way you wish – John uses a light blue and then a dark blue gloss. If the dark blue top coat is kept relatively thin then the light blue undercoat will show through to highlight the tops of the waves realistically. Naturally, the colours used can vary with the subject; neither the 'Arctic Ocean' for a frigate on the Murmansk convoy run, nor the 'Mekong' for a Vietnam riverine craft, would be sparkling Caribbean blue. As the DAS doesn't always stick too well to the styrene base, John lifts the dried 'tile' of putty out of the base and spreads glue over the styrene before replacing it (he favours 'No Nails' for this). The model is then replaced and glued into the impression in the putty; on some occasions John cuts out the putty completely from the bottom of the impression and glues the ship model directly to the styrene base. After doing any necessary touching up to the paintwork, John finishes the display by making up a surround using wooden beading, stained or painted to choice.

Detail of the hangar space on HMS *Devonshire*, with a helicopter stowed inside.

LEFT HMS *Cumberland*, a much-enhanced Airfix kit, in Far East waters. Note the addition of the junk model; one or more smaller craft, such as a launch or pinnace scurrying around a warship at anchor, helps to fix the scale visually, which is obviously a problem with a single waterline model.

RIGHT A warship from the age of Imperial gunboat diplomacy: HMS *Nile*, scratch-built in 1/700th scale.

LEFT The mine-hunter HMS *Nurton*, scratch-built in 1/600th scale.

RIGHT Work in progress: this is what scratch-building in 1/600th scale actually means. This is a Heinkel He60 floatplane for the *Graf Spee* under construction; the blob of Blu-Tack is holding one of the floats to be attached. The 50 pence coin measures 28mm corner to corner.

# Steve Zaloga

Steve Zaloga's encyclopaedic knowledge and high level of skill in the modelling of AFVs have earned him countless awards and a well-deserved reputation on both sides of the Atlantic as one of the masters in the modelling world, whose expertise is matched by his unselfishness in the sharing of his knowledge. For this book he has provided the following notes and photo captions on the display of his models:

'I almost always attach my finished tank models to a scenic base. I think that this helps to establish the model in its historical context, and the base helps to protect the model from handling. Most of my bases start as an inexpensive photo frame bought at my local arts-and-crafts store, which in my neighborhood in Maryland is part of the Michael's chain. The basic element is a sheet of synthetic material that will not warp; for many years I used Plexiglas, but I have been starting to use home insulation foam. The actual surface varies from model to model, sometimes using aftermarket materials such as resin cobblestones, but often Apoxie Sculpt epoxy putty, which is less subject to warping with age. The surface treatments depend on the subject, but I do spend a lot of money with Scenic Express in Pennsylvania, who carry a wide range of scenic materials aimed at model railroaders.

'Once my model is finished, I usually photograph it against a sheet of coloured art paper or simply against white paper. Since the ultimate aim of modelling is to recreate history, I also create a digital photographic illustration by photographing my model against a plain white background, importing the image into Adobe Photoshop, removing the plain background, and layering an actual photo below to create a scene.'

'This is a 1/35th-scale M4 Sherman model that I built for an Osprey book, *Modelling the US Army M4 75mm Sherman Medium Tank*. The first photo shows it on its scenic base, starting with a picture frame, a layer of Plexiglas with a sheet of resin cobblestones epoxied to it, and a wall and sidewalk from aftermarket resin bits. The M4 is finished as a Sherman of the 8th Tank Battalion, 4th Armored Division, in summer 1944; the background to the second photo is one I took in lower Normandy, in the countryside south of Omaha Beach.'

'This is the Tamiya 1/48th-scale Crusader on its scenic base, in this case a disc of house insulation foam with the edges smoothed using acrylic wood putty, and the desert surface created with Apoxie Sculpt epoxy putty. The two figures are from the excellent Dartmoor series; I usually add figures to the model as they help to convey the scale. This project was covered in more detail in *Military Modelling* magazine (Vol. 37 No. 8, 2007). The tank is depicted at the time of Operation *Battleaxe* in June 1941, finished in the distinctive Caunter camouflage scheme. The Crusader behind it in the second photo is another shot of the same model, taken at a different angle to help create the illusion of perspective'.

'The Academy M3 medium tank kit is displayed on a wooden photoframe base with the desert terrain modelled using a few layers of insulation foam with Apoxie Sculpt for the surface. This project was covered in more detail in *Military Modelling* magazine (Vol. 36 No. 9, 2006). In the second photo the M3 of 2/13th Armored in Tunisia in 1943 is displayed against a background photo that I actually took some years ago on the UAE Army's Maqatra range while attending a tank firing demonstration.'

'This was another Osprey modelling book project, based around a conversion of the 1/35th-scale Dragon Sherman kit. The base is the usual Plexiglas/Apoxie Sculpt combination, while the wall in the background is a plaster item from the Farina Enterprises diorama series. This M4A3 of the 2nd Armd Div is finished as it appeared during Operation *Grenade* in the Rhineland in February 1945. The photo background was shot out my front door when a particularly violent storm passed through the area, providing a very dramatic sky.'

'A 3rd Armd Div T26E1 Super Pershing on the prowl in Germany in April 1945. This project was covered in more detail in *Military Modelling* magazine (Vol. 35 No. 4, 2005). I wanted a slightly more dramatic base for this and used a particularly long photo frame; I built up the base from balsa foam covered with some acrylic texture gels to seal it and give it a more natural texture. The photo background is a farm scene from western Maryland.'

LEFT 'The reason I use Plexiglas or insulation foam is best explained by this photo of a small 1/35th-scale vignette that I built many years ago. I used a small sheet of plastic for the base, but over time it warped badly, as can be seen below the jeep. Actually, this photo was taken after I had already used a dry-wall screw to remove most of the warping in the center.'

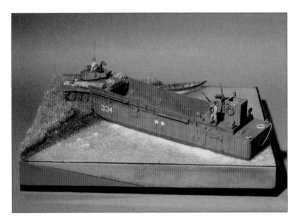

RIGHT AND BELOW 'This 1/72-scale diorama recreating a scene from the Rhine crossings of March 1945 was built using the Dragon LCM kit and the old and awful Hasegawa M24. To depict the water, I used a clear plastic 8 x 10-inch box picture frame with the inside tinted murky green, and the water surface textured using gloss acrylic gels. The shoreline and river bottom were made from plastic sheet and putty. This project was covered in more detail in *Military Modelling* magazine (Vol. 35 No. 5, 2005). The scenic background for the low-angle shot of the LCM-3 disgorging the Chaffee was actually photographed near my home, on the Chesapeake Bay.' (All photos courtesy Steve Zaloga)

# Rob Hendon

Robin Hendon is not only an award-winner, he is also one of the most prolific modellers I've ever met. While most of us favour a particular scale or subject area, be it tanks, aircraft, figures or fantasy, Rob never seems to put any limits on his modelling – if there's a kit of it, he'll build it. Rob works mostly with acrylic paints and, like Geoffrey Illsley and several other modellers whose work is featured in this book, he makes much use of Iwata airbrushes.

A 120mm figure of a dismounted dragoon of Napoleon's army in Egypt, 1798–1801. Note the carved detail on the ruined wall.

The crew of a late-war PzKpfw V Panther making a hasty bale-out during a city street-battle. This type of 'full diorama' presentation demands a wide range of modelling and painting skills, and getting realistic 'city rubble' is much more demanding than it might appear.

LEFT Deutsches Afrika Korps soldier, with little green friend. The two cans are another nice touch, but only because Rob has taken the trouble to get the stencilled markings absolutely right.

RIGHT 90mm figure of a 1917–18 assault battalion 'stormtrooper' from Miniature Alliance, about to heave a heavy 'concentrated charge' of wired-together stick grenades over a parapet. There are two good points to mention here. Firstly, the stance is realistic for a man trying trying to throw something weighing about 3lbs as far as he can; and secondly, the stance and the 'trench parapet' groundwork are in harmony. (Note, too, the nice root detail on the earth surface.)

ABOVE Close-up of a BAR gunner with the US 1st Ranger Bn, 1944, against the background of a Normandy coastal cliff.

ABOVE This Waffen-SS officer, a 90mm Pegaso kit, is skilfully integrated with a photographed forest background.

RIGHT This Gloster Gladiator biplane is a 1/48th-scale Roden kit. The pilot has been lifted from a picture of another aircraft by the magic of Adobe Photoshop.

The World War I flying ace Werner Voss in front of his Fokker Dr I. The triplane is a 1/32nd-scale Roden kit and the figure of Voss is by Mike Good of the Model Cellar.

Rob's 1/48th-scale Tamiya Swordfish, photographed on the slipway from a nicely dramatic angle.

A quarter-scale bust of a wealthy Anglo-Saxon warrior of c.AD 800.

'After the Battle': an Andrea 1/9th-scale resin bust of a footsoldier of about 1250. Both the helmet and sword are white metal.

A beautifully painted 1/9th-scale Warriors figure of a World War II US tanker in the turret of his Sherman.

This Waffen-SS Panther tank commander is a modified 1/6th-scale Tamiya figure with a head and cap from Rob's spares box.

Unfortunately I don't have a picture that shows the entire length of the Andrea U-boat, but this close-up of the 'interesting bit' of a boat of the 9. U-Flotille out of Brest gives an idea of Rob's presentation of this great waterline model.

'Herr Ka-Leu': the Andrea 1/9th-scale bust of a Kapitän-Leutnant U-boat commander in typical pose, leaning on the handle of the attack periscope. (All photos courtesy Rob Hendon)

ABOVE & BELOW 1/6th-scale figures such as these from the Dragon 'Action' series – an imposing-looking *grognard* of Napoleon's Imperial Guard, and a Falklands War-period British paratrooper – offer their own opportunities and challenges for model finishing and presentation. Their size and articulation invite a good deal of satisfying super-detailing and animation, but the behaviour of their fabric uniforms over limb joints makes it difficult to achieve a true scale effect in close-up photography.

# 'Spud' Murphy

After having spent some time enjoying the high life visiting such fun tourist spots as downtown Sierra Leone, Iraq, Kosovo and Afghanistan in a Hercules C130 (affectionately known in the RAF as 'Fat Albert'), Spud is now flying a desk as editor of *Model Military International*. Between times he builds models, including many of the display pieces seen on the Accurate Armour stand at the shows this company attends.

'Ambush on the Road to Poteau'. Spud's Ardennes diorama recreates the well-known photos showing soldiers of SS-PzGren Regt 1 looting vehicles abandoned (some so hastily that the engines were still running) by the US 14th Cavalry Group on 18 December 1944. The M21 mortar-carrier half-track is an old Tamiya kit, as is the Schwimmwagen. The jeep and trailer are from Italeri, and the Waffen-SS Panzergrenadier figures are all from Dragon.

'Somewhere in Normandy': a Firefly of 13th/18th Hussars (identifiable by the regimental serial '51' and the 27th Armd Bde's 'Pregnant Pilchard' seahorse insignia) grinds past a PaK 40 anti-tank gun hastily abandoned at a street corner, while infantry move forwards, alert for diehard defenders and snipers in the houses. The PaK is the Dragon kit and the Firefly, also by Dragon, has been improved with a Formations turret and detailing update kit.

ABOVE All the figures used in this diorama are by Dragon with the exception of the lance-corporal carrying the Sten gun, which is from the Canadian company Ultracast.

RIGHT 'Danger in the Hedgerow': Tommies ignore the temptations offered by this abandoned SdKfz 234/4 heavy armoured car in Normandy. The sign and tape discouraging souvenir-hunters are the sort of simple but authentic period touch that immediately turns a model vehicle and a few figures into a coherent 'story'.

'Iwo Jima': a US Marine Corps Sherman gives cover to a flamethrower team advancing through the volcanic desolation. Having modelled a large number of different marks of Sherman, Spud found that he could build this diesel-engined M4A2 literally from the spares box. The 'story' here is the vulnerability of tanks to suicidal close-range attack by Japanese infantry with hand-placed charges. The Sherman has track plates added to the turret and glacis as extra protection, wooden planks along the sides to frustrate magnetic AT charges, and nails welded points up to the hatch covers for the same purpose. The level of detail that Spud has added even extends to a good-luck horseshoe nailed to the side planks below the painted name 'Bad News'.

LEFT & BELOW Overall views of Spud's arrangement of the different elements of the model on the base; the black sand groundwork and small tree debris are backed up by careful study of photos of the arid, shell-ploughed terrain of Iwo Jima in March 1945.

The 'punchline' of the visual story: the outclassed Japanese tank that should have resisted the landings is a battered hulk, but a last-ditch defender lies in wait behind it, hoping to sell his life dearly by ramming a pole-charge against the Sherman while its accompanying Marine infantry are distracted. The Type 97 medium *Chi-Ha* is a Tamiya kit to which Model Kasten tracks have been added to give the realistic sag of heavy metal; the US figures are from Dragon, and the Japanese figure is an old one from Tamiya.

LEFT & BELOW Impressively detailed diorama of a British Sherman being serviced in a railway scrapyard, together with the service crew's Scammell Pioneer truck. The appeal of positioning the modelled scene obliquely on the base is immediately obvious here – and so is the extra care that Spud Murphy has taken with the railway 'backstop', which adds far more than the lazy option of a plain wall. The Tamiya M4 Sherman kit has added armour and detailing; the heap of rusting scrap beyond it was made up with bits from the spares box and scrap brass etch fret.

ABOVE 'Take a break, lad'. From this angle we get a hint of the care and skill of the detailing inside the Sherman's open engine hatches – the same is true of the detail visible through the turret hatches, though it is invisible here.

RIGHT The Scammell Pioneer 'wrecker' is a resin kit from Accurate Armour. This very realistic shot taken in the sunny open air perfectly demonstrates the enhanced realism that can be achieved by using natural light for model photography. Providing the foreground and background can be made convincing by cropping and a backdrop, photos taken from such low angles can often create a more dramatic and lifelike effect.

BELOW Spud's painstaking additions of miscellaneous equipment (and note the 'liberated' crate of bottles).

# A selection of prizewinners from EuroMilitaire 2008

LEFT In Class 16 for Military Vehicle Vignettes 'The Gallant Defeat', an Arnhem scenario by German modeller Günther Sternberg, was awarded a commendation by the judges. Street-fighting is a very demanding but dramatic setting for a diorama; showing battle-damage and combat soldiers in a setting of still basically intact suburban domesticity, with which the viewer automatically identifies, provides a sharp visual contrast.

RIGHT Also commended, in the class for Miscellaneous Civilian Subjects, was 'Black Saturday' by Andrew Norman. This extremely imaginative display idea incorporates bomb damage – a dramatic consequence of the Luftwaffe's 'Adler Angriff' air assault on London – bursting through the charred pages of a history book open at an account of the raids of 7 September 1940.

LEFT 'The Day of Peter Beach' was a large and very busy 1/35th-scale diorama centred on a British Tank Landing Ship being unloaded at an Italian dockside, flanked by a landing craft and a DUKW. Built by Italian modellers Fabrizio Faggion and Giacomo dal Santo, it was awarded a silver medal in Class 15 for Military Vehicle Dioramas. The LST bows are scratch-built, with internal detailing and lighting effects built into the vehicle deck (invisible here). The presentation of this large and complex subject is boldly straightforward, with everything emerging towards the viewer from a plain backdrop, and its success depends on sheer modelling skill.

LEFT 'StuG III Ausf G, MinenKommando Danmark' by Staf Snyers from Belgium won a gold medal. This is an interesting variation on the perenially-popular but challenging theme of a wrecked AFV, set in well planned and skilfully executed groundwork with a good water effect.

'Best of show' at EuroMilitaire 2008 was awarded to Marijn Van Gils for this surreal and wonderfully realized idea, in which 'display' could be said to be as central an element as the modelling skill of 'Van Gils Construction' (note the sign on the rear staging). When you realize that this monumental 'statue' emerging from a Magic Sculpt epoxy putty rock pinnacle is a 54mm figure – shorter than a cigarette – the extreme miniaturization of everything surrounding it suddenly snaps into perspective. The wheelbarrows are scratch-built from paper stiffened with liquid superglue, thin copper wire, and a wheel punched from plastic sheet; the railway wagons are built from scratch using plastic card and bits of photo-etched metal. The tiny cables, such as those from the

crane suspending the sword blade, are stretched sprue. All the scaffolding was scratch-built from brass wire, plastic sheet and leftover photo-etched details, with some 1/700th scale ship-modelling frets for things like stairs, ladders and railings; the plastic screens are ordinary cling-wrap covered with matt varnish and some brown washes. The 2.5mm-tall people are 1/700th-scale ship-modelling photo-etched figures, posed and thickened with liquid superglue and baking powder; they are painted with highlights and shadows to emphasize their 3D effect, and attached to the scaffolding with superglue and matt varnish. (All photos courtesy Adrian Hopwood/*Military Modelling*/EuroMilitaire)

## Spencer Pollard

Spencer Pollard has to fit his modelling in as best he can between his duties as the busy editor of *Military in Scale* magazine, but his efforts were rewarded at EuroMilitaire with a gold medal for this wonderfully busy scene, 'One Man's Junk'. A full-length article on the build had appeared in the magazine; then, before EuroMilitaire, the model was virtually destroyed in transit by an airline and had to be rebuilt in time to enter, so this is the Mk II version.

RIGHT TOP & BOTTOM The painstakingly rebuilt diorama 'One Man's Junk' depicts a vehicle-restorer's dream – a World War II Jagdpanzer 38(t) Hetzer surviving in the corner of a present-day junkyard.

BELOW Detail of the Hetzer's mantlet and glacis plate, showing Spencer's beautifully reproduced finish of faded paint traces over rusted metal. Using paints that have a different sheen from their neighbours makes any model more interesting than if it is painted overall in a consistent finish.

The loader, and a close-up of its bucket. This is weathered using multiple layers of MIG Productions' pigments, and a rub-over with graphite applied with both a cottonbud and a finger.

It took Spencer almost a week to assemble and paint all these individual bits of junk for the diorama.

The air vent and chimney were sprayed with a dark brown acrylic shade and then stippled while still wet with rusty pigments from the MIG Productions range. Once dry, further colours were worked into the surface of each piece until the effect was one of old rusty iron. Individual tiles were cut from a sheet of black Plasticard and then laid onto a thin sheet of white card cut to match the profile of the plaster block. (All photos courtesy Spencer Pollard)

# David Maddox

David began modelling at the age of six, but only started to concentrate on figures in the year 2000. He is a judge at EuroMilitaire and has won a number of awards, including golds. These examples of his work show how much appeal can be added to single figures by giving real thought and care to their display.

RIGHT 'Avalonian Trooper'. I particularly like the way David has modified the wooden base by cutting and colouring Plasticard to look like metal strapping. It gives the whole thing an authentically mediaeval air, with a shape reminiscent of a rigid quiver for crossbow bolts, or an early gunpowder flask.

ABOVE 'The Last Supper'. The additional details on the firing-step, allowed by the slight off-set of the figure, are just right – not too little, not too much.

'Across a Nightingale Floor.' A Japanese samurai in everyday clothing is posed on an impression of one of the 'anti-*ninja*' wooden floors constructed in *daimyo*'s castles to betray the approach of would-be assassins by giving out telltale creaking sounds.

'Mameluke'. To get the balance of this sort of display right – conveying a context without overwhelming the figure itself – takes a great deal more care than might appear. The architectural detail looks convincing, and the colour palette is sympathetic to that of the warrior's costume.

A science-fiction figure, 'The Pilot' is a simple piece beautifully finished. The subdued colours and the black painting of the underside of the bust draw your eye straight to the face, while the clean, textured disc from which it rises delicately conveys an impression of a technological culture.

In contrast to the space-pilot, David's hobbit-like 'Yarry' looks out at us from a suitably 'organic' groundwork setting in autumnal colours. (All photos courtesy David Maddox)

# Haris Ali

RIGHT In his 'Desert Encounter', Haris has come up with a novel way of combining an aircraft and a vehicle both in their natural elements. The two kits he used are the Tamiya 1/48th-scale Fieseler Fi156C Storch and Crusader Mk III. This photo shows how the aircraft was supported above the rockface – the acrylic rod is just visible behind the port undercarriage leg. The prop of the Storch is being spun using a small hairdryer.

ABOVE The base was constructed in two parts, with a box made from foam board fixed at the back to support the Woodland Scenics' rockface of the desert escarpment. The box incorporated a piece of square-section styrene that would later house a length of clear acrylic rod onto which the aircraft would be mounted.

BELOW 'What the *#@!?..' The startled crew of the Crusader. The figures are by ArtofWar from their Squad 48 range, with minor adjustments: Haris removed the heads, shaved a bit off the necks and re-attached them with Milliput, tilted back to stare upwards in alarm.

ABOVE I must admit that I took a small liberty with the last picture and removed the rod in Photoshop – Haris' work made it irresistible. (All photos courtesy Haris Ali)

# Appendix

Naturally, several of the UK shops listed below are those local to me in South-East England, but enquiries to the manufacturers of the various products will help readers in other parts of the country to find suppliers. Most of those listed also provide a catalogue and mail-order service. If calling from overseas add (0044) to the beginning of the telephone number, and drop the first (0) of the area code.

## Materials, tools, etc.; UK

*Historex Agents, Wellington House, 157 Snargate Street, Dover, Kent CT17 9BZ*
*tel: 01304-206720 fax: 01304-204528*
*email: sales@historex-agents.co.uk*
*website: www.historex-agents co.uk*
Supplier of the two Historex Punch & Die sets for forming rivets and studs, and of a wide range of figures from all the major names including Hornet, Wolf, Andrea and Verlinden.

*The Airbrush Co Ltd, Unit 7, Marlborough Road East, Lancing Business Park, Lancing, W. Sussex BN15 8UF*
*tel: 01903-767800*
*email: sales@airbrushes.com*
*website: www.airbrushes.com*
The Airbrush Company carry the complete range of Iwata airbrushes and also the Lifecolour range of paints; their range of products suits everyone from beginner to expert.

*LSA Models, 151 Sackville Road, Hove, E. Sussex BN3 3HD*
*tel: 01273-705420*
*email: orders@lsamodels.co.uk*
*website :www.lsamodels.co.uk*
For Tamiya weathering compounds including their excellent 'Mud Stick', CMK weathering powders, Warrior Custom Dioramics, static grasses and Mod-Roc plaster bandage, as well as a large range of plastic and resin kits.

*Sylmasta, PO Box 262, Haywards Heath, West Sussex, RH16 2FR*
*tel: 01444-415027 fax: 01444-458606*
*email: Sales@Sylmasta.com*
*website: www.sylmasta.com*
This company markets a large range of epoxy putties, adhesives, casting materials, etc., and their online catalogue is well worth looking at.

*Perry Miniatures, PO Box 6512, Nottingham NG7 1UJ*
*tel: 01159-168307*
*e-mail: perryminiatures@aol.com*
*website: www.perry-miniatures.com*
The Perrys market a wide range of excellent white-metal wargaming figures.

*4D Modelshop Ltd, The Arches, 120 Leman Street, London E1 8EU*
*tel: 020-7264-1288*
*email: info@modelshop.co.uk*
*website: www.modelshop.co.uk*

4D carries a huge range of modelling materials – wood, plastics, paper, fibre optics and metal – and also a number of excellent groundwork products by Green Scene such as 'Flexibark', miniature leaves marketed under the name of 'The Little Leaf Co', and resins for making bodies of water. To see the full range, download their free catalogue.

*Scale Link Ltd., Unit 19B, Applins Farm Business Centre,*
*Farrington, Dorset DA11 8RA*
*tel/fax: 01747-811817*
*email: info@scalelink.co.uk*
*website: www.scalelink.co.uk*
A wide range of white-metal figures and accessories, and an equally large choice of fine brass etched foliage and equipment. Also resin detailing parts and full resin kits. Catalogue available for downloading.

*Alex Tiranti*
*(Mail order & showroom) 3 Pipers Court, Berkshire Drive, Thatcham, Berkshire RG19 4ER*
*(London shop) 27 Warren Street, London W1T 5NB*
*tels: 0845-123-2100 (mail order); 020-7636-8565 (London shop)*
*email: enquiries@tiranti.co.uk*
*website: www.tiranti.co.uk*
Materials, supplies and equipment for home casting; catalogue available.

*Gaugemaster Controls plc, Gaugemaster House, Ford Road, Arundel, W. Sussex BN18 0BN*
*tel: 01903-884488*
*website: www.gaugemaster.com*
Main stockists of Noch, Faller, Peco and Jordan, as well as Preiser figures, and their own range of groundcovers.

*Great North Roads, 9A Marcombe Road, Torquay, Devon TQ2 6LL*
*tel: 01803-400436*
*mobile: 07900-985328*
*email: svfarrugia@yahoo.co.uk*
Maker and supplier of ceramic castings of buildings, roads, etc. These are far superior to the old plaster diorama castings; the detailing is sharp and the ceramic is much tougher. They need no undercoating before painting, and you can use acrylics or enamels. *NB mail order only.*

*Cammett Ltd, Unit 5, Forest Road, Greenfield Industrial Estate, Hay-on-Wye, Hereford HR3 5FA*
*tel: 01497-822757*
*email: cammettco@btinternet.com*
Modelling supplies specialist, with a comprehensive range of tools as well as all the products needed to finish the model, including Lifecolour paints, White Ensign Colourcoats and Alclad II. Cammett now also carry the Hold & Fold range, Cast-a-Coat, Snow-Coat & Ice-Coat. Pacific Coast Models is the US distributor for Cammett products; all orders received from the US in the UK for Cammett's own products will be redirected to Pacific Coast Models.

*Squires Model & Craft Tools, 100 London Road, Bognor Regis, W. Sussex PO21 1DD*
*tel: 01243-842424*
*email: sales@squirestools.com*
A mail-order company which also has stalls at shows, with a huge range of products for the modeller. Send for one of their catalogues – it's well worth it.

*Just Bases, 21 Graham Road, Paignton, Devon, TQ3 1BB*
*tel: 01803- 558520*
*email: paul@just-bases.co.uk.*
*website: www.just-bases.co.uk*
Suppliers of a variety of wooden bases.

*Stan Britnell Bases*
*tel: 01304-214032 for enquiries – visitors by appointment only*
Stan makes these bases as a sideline but, as you can see from the ones
pictured in the 'Bases and cases' section of this book, they are of extremely
high quality.

### Reference books; UK
The following companies carry a very full stock of books that would provide
useful reference to nearly all modellers.

*Historex Agents, Wellington House, 157, Snargate Street,Dover, Kent CT17 9BZ*
*tel: 01304-206720 fax: 01304-204528*
*email: sales@historex-agents.co.uk*
*website: www.historex-agents co.uk*
Suppliers of a number of reference books and magazines including my two
Osprey Masterclass titles *Terrain Modelling* and *Advanced Terrain Modelling*, the
magazine *Military Miniatures in Review*, and publications by Euro Modelisimo
and Andrea, all of which are rich sources for diorama ideas.

*Aviation Book Centre, PO Box 4413, Atherstone, Warwickshire CV9 9AS*
*tel: 0845-2604413*
*email: sales@aviationbookcentre.com*
*website: www.aviationbookcentre.com*
Despite the name this company covers much more than aviation, stocking
reference books on most military subjects.

*The Avid Reader, Unit 10, Hodfar Road, Sandy Lane Industrial Estate,*
*Stourport, Worcestershire DY13 9QB*
*tel: 01299-823330*
*e-mail: info@bookworldws.co.uk*
Another company with a huge range of good reference books.

*Osprey Publishing, Midland House, West Way, Botley, Oxford OX2 0PH*
*tel: (general enquiries) 01865-727022*
*email: customerservice@ospreypublishing.com*
*website: ospreypublishing.com*
Publishers of the 'Men-at-Arms', 'Elite', 'New Vanguard', 'Fortress', 'Campaign'
and 'Aircraft of the Aces' series running to many hundreds of titles, among
other publications.

*Casemate UK, 17 Cheap Street, Newbury, Berkshire RG14 5DD*
*tel: 01635-231091*
*email: casemate-uk@casematepublishing.co.uk*
*website: www.casematepublishing.co.uk*
This company runs a list of military reference books that cover a span from
mediaeval times to the 21st century.

# Materials, tools, etc.; USA
When calling the USA from the UK, add (001) before the dialling code.

*Woodland Scenics, PO Box 98, Linn Creek, MO 65052*
*tel: (573) 346-5555 fax: (573) 346-3768*
*website: www.woodlandscenics.com*
Producers of first-class groundwork materials for the railroad modeller, but
which are equally good for the diorama builder. They carry a very large range,
all under their own brand name; they also publish *The Scenery Manual*, an
excellent 'how-to' book – as well as a version on video – covering how to
make the best of their products.

*Timberline Scenery, PO Box 57, Platville, CO 80651*
*tel: ( 970) 785-0321*
*website: www.timberlinescenery.com*
Makers of the excellent 'Weather-Rite' weathering agent for 'old timber,' this
company also sells a range of trees and ground covers, in particular their very
useful 'forest floor litter'.

*Micro-Mark, 340 Snyder Avenue, Berkley Heights, NJ 07922-1595*
*tel: (800) 225-1066*
*website: www.Micro-Mark.com*
One of the best suppliers of a wide range of tools for the modeller, plus scenic
materials and weathering agents. Full catalogues available.

*Scenic Express Inc, 175 Sheffield Drive #100, Delmont, PA 15626*
*tel: toll-free sales (800) 234-9995 (US & Canada customers only)*
*sales: (724) 468-3106   fax: (724) 468-3879*
*email: sales@scenicexpress.com*
*website: www.scenicexpress.com*
This company handles several of the best makes of grasses, foliage, leaves,
flocks and turf from Noch, Woodland Scenics, Silflor and Heki, as well as
products of their own.

*Miller Engineering, PO Box 282, New Canaan, CT 06903*
*tel: (203) 595-0619*
*email: milleren@microstru.com*
*website: microstru.com*
This company sells miniature lighting for modellers.

## Websites

*www.scalemodelindex.com*
An enormous site put together by Tony Matteliano, which lists practically
any club, supplier or information site that could possibly be of interest to a
modeller. If it's not here, it probably doesn't exist.

*www.armorama.com.*
Large site with many links, mostly as the name implies for the AFV modeller.

*www.missing-lynx.com*
Another informative site with good links to the rest of the modelling world.

*www.monroeperdu.com*
This company markets excellent accessories and printed work for the
diorama builder.

*www.kitmaker.net*
A very good site for those of you looking for a particular manufacturer or a
particular kit.

# Index